Children's Ballet Dictionary

An Illustrated Guide

Judy John-Baptiste

Table of Contents

This pictorial dictionary is designed to assist ballet pupils in learning the terms that are used in ballet grades and ballet in general. It is also a resource for parents to use when helping their children practise at home. The ballet terms are organised in alphabetical order, many of which are accompanied by clear illustrations. Most of the exercises are described using fifth position of the feet but may be performed using third position.

Adage

Slow

Dance movements that are performed at a slow pace.

Alignment

A term used to describe the placement of a dancer's body in relation to stage directions.

Allegro

A lively dance sequence comprised of jumps. There are three types of allegro: petit allegro, medium allegro and grand allegro

Allongé

Extended

An extended line normally associated with arabesque.

Arabesque 1st 2nd 3rd

A dance pose where the dancer is standing on one leg. The gesturing leg is extended back at a 90 degree angle with palms facing down. The arabesque pose can be performed in a variety of ways including allongé and penché.

À *terre*

On the ground

A position where the working leg maintains contact with the floor via the toe.

Attitude

A body position

A pose on one leg where the working leg is lifted and bent at an angle. The knee is normally held higher than the foot and can be performed devant or derriere, en pointe or en relevé.

Assemblé (pas)

To assemble

A jump that starts with the feet in 5th position. A demi plié is performed followed by the back or front leg sliding out to degagé 2nd. The supporting leg pushes off the floor followed by the gesturing leg closing in a tight 5th position in the air before landing in 5th position. Assemblé can be performed in all directions. When assemblé turns without a jump it is called assemblé soutenu en tournant.

Balancé

To sway

A lilting step in ¾ timing. Balancé is performed by the weight transferring from one foot to the other three times. It can be performed in all directions including en tournant.

Barre

A horizontal pole used for support at the beginning of a ballet class.

Battu

Beaten

The batterie group of jumps. Any jump performed with a beat action caused by the calves crossing en l'air.

Changement (de pieds)
Changing

A jump from 3rd or 5th position where the feet changes position in the air before landing.

Chassé
Chased or hunted

Chassé is a sliding action starting in 5th demi plié. The working leg slides in any direction to 4th or to 2nd position. Chassé are also performed as jumps.

Chassé Jumps

Classical Walks

A graceful transference of weight from one foot to the other.

Corps (de ballet)
Body

A body of dancers who are not performing soloists.

Coté (de)
To or from the side.

Cou de pied
Neck of the foot

Position of the working foot placed above the ankle bone of the supporting leg. Both legs are turned out with the gesturing leg placed devant or derrière. The gesturing leg may be pointed, flexed or "wrapped" around the ankle.

Coupé

Cut (to)

The action of transferring (cutting) the weight of one foot to the other. The action may start from 5th position in demi plié, tendu devant or à la seconde. Coupé may be performed à terre or as a jump (coupé sauté)

Coupé Sauté

Coupé sauté is performed as a jump when the weight is transferred from one leg to the other.

Couru

To run

A dainty running step with the feet close together. Couru can be performed in 5th or 1st in all directions. When performed in 1st position the feet are mostly in parallel. In 5th position the legs travel crossed led by the front foot.

Croisé

Crossed

A position where the legs are crossed at an angle facing a downstage diagonal to the left or right. Croisé may be performed derrière or devant.

Curtsey

A female bow taken at the end of class or performance.

Degagé (battement)

Released

Degagé refers to the disengagement of the working leg to the front, side or back with toes toe maintaining contact with the floor.

Demi Detourné

Half turned way

A swivel turn starting in fifth position where a half turn is performed towards the direction of the back foot. At the completion of the turn the feet have exchanged positions.

Derrière

Behind, from the back.

Used to describe the position of the foot or an action starting from the back.

Dessous

Under

Action where the working foot passes or closes behind the supporting leg.

Dessus

Over, on top of

Action where the working leg passes or closes in front of the supporting leg.

Detourné

Turned away

A turn starting in fifth position plié where a swivel turn is performed towards the direction of the back foot. Upon completion of the turn the feet will have exchanged positions.

Devant

In front of, from the front.

Used to describe the foot positioned at the front or actions starting from the front foot.

Développé

Unfolded

A slow unfolding movement with the working leg starting from 5th position. Développé may be started from the devant, derrière or à la seconde.

Écarté

Separated

Écarté describes a dancer's alignment en diagonale where with the feet are in a tendu 2nd position either derriere or devant. Écarté can be taken en l'air.

Échappé

Escaped

Échappé is the action of moving from a closed position to 2ⁿᵈ or 4ᵗʰ position on relevé or en pointe.

Échappé Sauté

Escaped

A jump with two sautés. Échappé sauté starts from a closed position to an open position, and then back to a closed position. Échappé sauté starts from 5th or 1st position opening to 2nd or 4th. It then returns back to its staring point. Échappé can be performed en croix.

Efface

Shaded

A term used to describe a body alignment in an open position.

Enchainement

Linking

A collection of steps danced together.

En Croix

In the shape of a cross

A sequence that is repeated devant, à la seconde, derrière and back to seconde.

En L'air

In the air

Any action or position where the working leg is off the floor.

Entrechat

Interweaving

A jump from 5th position where the legs cross in the air to cause them to beat. An entrechat trois is performed with a jump from fifth position, the legs beat without changing position. Afterwards the legs change position before landing on one leg with the other in the cou de pied position. Entrechat quatre is performed when the jump from two feet changes position with a beat in the air and then lands in the original fifth position.

Épaulement
Shouldering

The action of rotating the upper torso through the back. The torso from the waist down is kept in place without being displaced.

Fondu (battement)
Melted

An action that can be started in 5th position or with the working leg extended. The working leg is bent bringing the foot to the cou de pied position whilst bending the supporting leg at the same time. Both legs are stretched to finish. Battement fondu can be performed devant, à la seconde or derrière.

Fouetté

Whipped

A rotation of the body away from a gesturing leg. The gesturing leg may be performed à terre or en l'air. A fouetté may be performed as a jump or turn.

Frappé (battement)
Struck (to strike)

A strong action where a flexed foot is placed in the cou de pied position of the supporting leg and extends either devant, à la seconde or derrière as it strikes the floor with the ball of the foot.

Gallop
A travelling jump loosely based on a posé followed by coupé sauté.

Gavotte
A court dance during the reign of Louis XIV.

Glissade

To glide

A gliding step that starts from 5th position and ends in fifth position. From demi plié 5th position, the working leg is released to en fondu. The weight of the body is transferred to the working leg, releasing the supporting leg to a degagé position which closes to form demi plié in fifth. Glissade may be performed in any direction and is often used as a linking step, or as a preparation for a jump.

Glissé (battement)
Glided

A sliding action taken from either 1st or 5th position. The foot slides along the floor and is released approximately an inch away from the floor. Battement glissé can be performed in all directions.

Grand (e)
Big, large as in grand battement.

Grand Battement
Large Beating

An action where the dancer throws the leg devant, derrière or à la seconde from 5th position. The movement passes through the tendu position and returns back to 5th position. At the barre grand battement is performed en crois.

Grande Jeté

A large leap from one leg to the other travelling en avant.

Petit Jeté

A small throw (throwing the weight from one leg to another)

Jeté Ordinaire

A jump from demi plié in 5th position where the working leg brushes to glissé 2nd. The weight is transferred to the working leg and the supporting leg finishes in the cou de pied position devant or derrière. There are a wide range of jetés from petit jeté, jeté en tournant and grand jeté.

Opposition

Opposition refers to the position of the arm being opposite to the leg in front. For instance if the right foot is positioned to the front in fifth position, the left hand would be positioned front or above with the right hand to the side.

Ouvert (en)
Open

Ouvert is used to describe an open body alignment where the legs are open in 2nd or 4th.

Ordinaire
Ordinary
A term to describe the basic version of a step.

Pas de Basque glissé
Basque step

Pas de Basque glissé is a step in ¾ timing that transfers the weight from one foot to the other. It starts from 5th position, the working leg is released to the front en fondu. The leg rotates to 2nd en fondu then the weight is transferred onto the working leg en fondu. The extended leg passes through 1st in demi plié to 4th demi plié, degagé derrière and closes in 5th position derrière . Pas de Basque may be performed as a jump known as pas de Basque sauté.

Pas de Bourrée

Step

Pas de bourrée is a series of linked steps that travel transferring the weight on the feet three times. It can be performed in all directions with a variety of configurations.

Pas de Chat

Step of the Cat

A jump that starts and ends in 5th position. The right or left foot starts derriere and withdraws to the side of the opposite knee which is followed by the supporting leg withdrawing in quick succession. In pas de chat the feet do not change.

Pas de Cheval
Step of the horse

The step starts with the working leg pointed in an open position. It then brushes towards the supporting leg performing a small développé before returning back to the starting position. Pas de cheval may be performed in all directions, but often starts devant.

Pas de Valse
Waltz Step
A lyrical dance step in ¾ timing

Passé

Passed (to go pass)

A term used to describe the working leg passing the supporting leg from one position to another. The working leg moves from front to back, or from back to front.

Penché

Inclined

An action that is tilted at an angle.

Pirouette

A turn on one leg with the working leg in the retiré position. A pirouette can be performed en dedans or dehors. Many turns can be performed in one pirouette en pointe or on demi pointe.

Plié: Grand Plié Demi Plié
Demi Plié
Half bend

Demi plié refers to a half bend of the knees with the heels on the floor. The legs are turned out with the knees positioned over the toes. Demi plié is the foundation for all jumps. Demi plié is performed in all five positions of the feet with the heels keeping contact with the floor.

Grand Plié

Large bend

Grand plié is a large bending of the knees with the heels coming of the floor in all positions except for second position. The feet are turned out with the knees bending in line with toes.

Polka

A lively dance in 2/4 timing that became the national dance of Czechoslovakia.

Port de Bras

Carriage of the arms

A choreographic sequence that uses the standard positions of the arms.

Posé

Poised

A transference of weight stepping onto one foot from the other to form a posed position on one leg. The transition may be to relevé, à terre or en pointe from battement fondu or glissé.

Positions of the Arms

Hands on Waist

Bras Bas

First Position

Demi Second Position

Second Position

Third Position

Fourth Position

Open Fifth Position

Fifth Position

Positions of the Feet

First Position   Second Position   Third Position

Fourth Position   Fifth Position   Sixth Position

À Terre   Demi Pointe   En Pointe

Relevé
Raised

Relevé is an action where the body is elevated onto demi pointe or pointe. It can be performed from a snatched action in demi plié or the heels coming progressively off the floor. Relevé can be performed from all the positions of the feet.

Retiré
Withdrawn (to pull up, withdraw)

An action that involves the working leg sliding the foot up the supporting leg to finish with the toes at the side of the knee. Retiré is performed starting from devant or derrière.

Retiré Passé

An action that slides the foot of the working leg up to the retiré position. The foot finishes at the back if it started at the front or vice versa.

Retiré Sauté

A spring with the gesturing leg simultaneously sliding up to the retiré position. The spring starts in 5th position with the working foot passing from devant to derrière or vice versa. Both feet are turned out and may be performed en avant or en arrière.

Reverence

A choreographed bow or curtsey performed at the end of a class or examination to thank the teacher or examiner.

Rond de Jambe

Circle of the leg

A rotation of the working leg starting from the front side or back. Rond de jambe is performed en dedans or en dehors. It is also performed à terre or en l'air.

Rotational Directions

En Dehors: Outward rotation away from the supporting leg

En Dedans: Inward rotation towards the supporting leg

Sauté

Jumped

A jump into the air with two legs that returns to the ground with two legs simultaneously. A sauté may be performed in all the positions but is mostly associated with 1st 2nd and 4th .

Sissonne Ordinaire

Scissors

A sissonne is a jump from two feet in 5th position landing on one foot. Sissonne ordinaire lands with one foot in the cou de pied position. Other variations are sissonne fermé and sissonne ouvert. Sissone fermé concludes with the working leg closing in demi plié in fifth position. Sissonne ouvert finishes with the working leg en l'air and the supporting leg in demi plié.

Soubresaut

To jolt

A jump starting from 5th position, landing back in 5th position without changing positions of the feet.

Soutenu (pas)

Sustained

A fifth position followed by degagé en fondu devant or derrière, closing back to fifth position.

Spring Points

A delicate leap on the spot from leg to the other with the working leg finishing in degagé devant. Spring points can also be performed as a hop on one leg and en tournant.

Sur Place

One the spot

Used to describe an action that remains in place and doesn't travel.

Temps Levé

Time raised

A hop on one leg with the other foot in a raised position.

Tarantella

An Italian folk dance in 6/8 timing.

Tendu (battement)

Stretched

A stretched or extended position where the foot extends from either 1st or 5th position. The foot slides along the floor until contact with the floor is maintained through the tips of the toes only. The foot then returns back to 1st or 5th position. Tendu may be performed to devant, derrière or à la seconde positions.

Tournant (en)

An action performed turning.

Travelling Directions

En Arrière: Travelling backwards (away from the audience).

En Avant: Travelling forwards (toward the audience).

En Diagonale: Travelling on a diagonal line.

www.teachingballetcreatively.com

Made in the USA
San Bernardino, CA
13 December 2018